GOLD, PEACE, AND PROSPERITY

GOLD, PEACE, AND PROSPERITY:
THE BIRTH OF A NEW CURRENCY

Second Edition

Ron Paul

MISES INSTITUTE

First printing 1981 by the Foundation for Rational Economics and Education

Pocket paperback edition Copyright © 2011 Ludwig von Mises Institute and published under the Creative Commons Attribution License 3.0. http://creativecommons.org/licenses/by/3.0/

Ludwig von Mises Institute
815 West Magnolia Avenue
Auburn, Alabama 36832
mises.org

ISBN: 978-1-61016-196-1

DEDICATION

To Carol, whose love and support
are more precious than gold.

CONTENTS

FOREWORD

IN THIS SHORT PAMPHLET, Congressman Ron Paul has written one of the most enlightening explanations of inflation that I have ever read. It is both a history and an analysis. That history goes back further than our Revolutionary War, but as a continuous narrative it begins, as it should, in 1913 and 1914.

In the first of those years the United States passed the Federal Reserve Act, which in addition to providing only a fractional gold cover for Federal Reserve notes and deposits, made it possible for the commercial banks to borrow from the newly created Federal Reserve Banks. They could thus increase their own loans, and therefore the "money supply" they could bring into being. This made inflation possible; but this fact was not generally recognized as long as gold convertibility of the outstanding paper currency was maintained.

What happened in 1914 was more obvious and more dramatic. World War I broke out, and the belligerents instantly suspended gold conversion of their currencies. Each nation did that for "self protection." Each belligerent knew that other countries would be unlikely to accept its paper currency at par, or would in any case immediately turn it in for gold. So each belligerent kept its gold supply as a final reserve, to be paid out only when other countries would accept no other means of payment.

After World War I, the belligerents eventually returned to a gold standard, but meanwhile they had enormously expanded their paper currency and raised their "price levels," and so were to suffer the drastic commodity price collapse of 1920 to 1921, and the crisis of 1929 to 1933.

But I do not wish to trench here on Dr. Paul's excellent account. When he comes to analysis, he shows that inflation is always the result of an increase in the money supply, either encouraged or initiated by government action. He not only points out that this money supply increase must be halted if we are to escape even greater economic devastation, but he makes clear why we are altogether unlikely to halt the increase until we return once more to a real gold standard.

One of the great merits of Congressman Paul's account is that it avoids all technicalities, and enables the reader to recognize step by step what has happened to us and how we can return to monetary and economic sanity.

— Henry Hazlitt

PREFACE

R ON PAUL IS A most unusual politician—in many ways. In the first place, he really knows what he's talking about. He is not only for the gold standard. He knows why he is for it, and he is familiar with the most advanced and complex economic insights on the true nature of inflation, on how inflation works, and how inflationary credit expansion brings about booms and busts. And yet Ron has the remarkable ability to take these complex and vital insights and to present them in clear, lucid, hard-hitting terms to the non-economist reader. His economics is as sound as a bell.

But, even more important, Ron Paul is an unusual politician because he doesn't simply pay lip service to moral principles. He believes in moral principles in his mind and heart, and he fights for them passionately and effectively. High on his set of moral principles is the vital importance of individual freedom, of the individual's natural right to be free of assault and aggression, and of his right to keep the property that he has earned on the free market, and not have it stolen from him by confiscatory taxes and government regulations.

Ron Paul, in short, is that rare American, and still rarer politician, who deeply understands and battles for the principles of liberty that were fought for and established by the Founding Fathers of this country. He understands that sound economics, moral principles, and individual freedom all go together, like a seamless web. They cannot be separated, and they stand or fall together.

Ron Paul understands that all three parts of this system of liberty have been under grave attack for decades, and that the main problem is the federal government itself. The government has systematically eroded and invaded property rights, has piled on ever higher taxes, ever more onerous regulations, and, most sinister because most hidden, has eroded the value of the dollar and of all of our savings through inflation. Ron Paul is an unusual politician because he is not content to shrug his shoulders, to "go with the flow," as Californians say, or to go along in order to get along. He is a man of honor as well as a man of principle, and so he has, ever since he got into politics, been doing something about it. He has fought, sometimes single-handedly, for our liberties and for our savings.

Inflation, as Ron Paul points out, is caused by the government's continual creation of new money, by what amounts to its system of legalized counterfeiting. But, if that is so, why not simply urge the government to stop the creation of money? Why not point out to our rulers the bad consequences of their actions? But Ron Paul realizes that this kind of education, or even pressure, is not going to work by itself. For we are dealing not simply with ignorant or misled people; we are dealing with a pernicious system.

Let us put it this way: give any man or group power, and it will tend to use that power. If the power is inherently abusive, then that power will be abused. Our present system gives to the federal government and its Federal Reserve System the unlimited power to counterfeit. The problem is that if the Fed has the power to counterfeit, it will inevitably use that power. Why? Because the power to counterfeit is too tempting. The power to create money means that it is far more tempting to print it than to work for it. It means that the counterfeiter can pay his debts, spend more money, give more money to his friends and associates. In the case of government, the power to counterfeit means that government's debts can be paid without levying taxes, that government spending can increase, and that political allies can be purchased and maintained.

The power to counterfeit is the power to abuse. It is not enough to urge the government to use it more moderately. The power must be taken away. Counterfeiting is fraud, and no one should have the right to counterfeit, least of all government, whose record of counterfeiting throughout history is black indeed. Money and banking must be separated from the State, just as Church and State are separated in the American tradition, just as the economy and the State should be separated.

Vital to this necessary reform is the return to a money which is a useful product produced by the free market itself. In every society, people on the market voluntarily arrive at one or two commodities which are the most useful to use as a money. For thousands of years, gold has been selected by count-less societies as that money. The only alternative to a market commodity-money is what we unfortunately have now: paper tickets issued by the government and called "money." Since the paper tickets—dollars, francs, pounds sterling, or what have you—are issued by the government, the government can issue any amount it arbitrarily chooses. Counterfeiting is built into the system, and hence so is inflation and eventual destruction of the currency.

The only genuine solution to the evil of inflation, then, is to separate money from the State, to make money once again a market commodity instead of a fiat ticket issued by the central government. The dollar must once again be what is was originally until it was, in effect, nationalized. The dollar must once again be simply a name for a unit of weight of gold coin. Only this kind of fundamental reform will cure the ravages of inflation. Because Ron Paul is one of the few men in public life who truly understands the problem and is willing to fight to cure it, it is truly a pleasure for me to write the preface to this booklet.

— *Murray N. Rothbard*

Impending Social Strife?

THE GREATEST THREAT facing middle and working class Americans is our depreciating paper currency.

At least when the kings of old debased their coinage, by adding copper to the precious metal, there was still some objective value to the resulting money. But as economist David Ricardo observed almost two centuries ago, when money costs nothing, it will become worth nothing.

"Government," said Ludwig von Mises, "is the only agency that can take a useful commodity like paper, slap some ink on it, and make it totally worthless."

Today, thanks to 67 years of central bank control over the money supply, we face an economic and political crisis greater than any we have faced before.

We probably will see widespread civil disorder in the 1980s, as a direct result of our faltering economic system. The dollar has been damaged by decades of interventionism, and Congress has legitimized depreciation of the dollar and forced redistribution of wealth through corporate and social welfare schemes.

All aspects of the interventionist system threaten freedom and social peace, but money is the major issue, since it is the lifeblood of all economic transactions. If we are to reverse the trends of the past six or seven decades, honest money and monetary debasement must become top concerns of ordinary Americans.

The late Martin Gilbert, head economist for a Swiss bank, was a convert to the gold standard. Among his employees was a young manual worker. "Once a month," said Gilbert, "he took part of his pay and bought a gold coin for his wife. I remonstrated with him about it once, and he said, 'Look, don't you Americans come over here and try to tell us how to live. I go home and I give that coin to my wife, and I tell her, "If something happens to me, and to the bank and all the governments, you can go into the countryside and give it to a farmer, and with that coin you can eat for a week."' I came around to the opinion that he knew something I didn't know."

THE PEOPLE ARE
DEMANDING AN
END TO INFLATION

THE RECENT CHAOS in the money markets is telling us that the world is rejecting the American dollar as a reserve currency, and agreeing with the young man in Martin Gilbert's story. Tragically, there is probably little future for the dollar, or dollar-denominated assets.

Because all other nations are inflating and therefore destroying their currencies, trading foreign currencies to protect against the ravages of a depreciating currency is also becoming less attractive. The alternative, as it has been throughout history, is to seek and hold real money: gold and silver.

Fifty years of systematic monetary destruction now threaten the existence of our constitutional republic. The American people are frightened by what they see, and they are demanding that the inflation stop. More citizens are realizing that Congress and the Federal Reserve have generated a flood of paper money with no intrinsic value.

It is rare to find anyone today who believes that wealth can come out of a printing press. The corporate bailouts, guaranteed loans, government contracts, and welfare gimmicks all have failed, and the people can no longer be duped.

Politicians who have been in office for too many years, and have therefore lost touch with the people, pay no heed to the rising clamor for money of real value. But the old scapegoats no longer work. Blaming Arabs, businessmen, labor unions, or consumers for rising prices doesn't drown out the steady hum of printing presses running 24 hours a day, ballooning the money supply, and thereby debasing every dollar previously printed. Congress alone is responsible for inflation, and Congress alone can stop it. It has shirked its responsibility for decades, but events are making a continuation impossible. It is time now to prepare for monetary reform.

DEPRECIATION IS NOTHING NEW

IN MARCO POLO's great book of travels, he talks about a coin called the bezant circulating in Kublai Khan's Mongol Chinese empire. The emperor, like the vast majority of politicians, found the lure of paper money irresistible. In his case, however, it was money printed on pieces of mulberry tree bark. The same disastrous effects, seen everywhere else in history, followed. Prices increased, and the gold bezant took on increasing importance for the people as the government debauched the irredeemable fiat currency. Abuse of paper money helped lead, notes Antony Sutton, to the expulsion of the Mongol dynasty from China. Government demands that the people accept printed mulberry bark as equivalent to metallic money had no effect.

A gold bezant, the major trading coin of Byzantium.

The bezant, however, was minted not by the Chinese, but by the Byzantine Empire. For ten centuries Byzantine coins were accepted all over the world, and Byzantium dominated trade for thousands of miles in every direction from Constantinople. Even the royal accounts of medieval England, says Dr. Sutton, were kept in bezants. The Byzantine Empire only declined when it debased the bezant, adding more cheap alloys and removing gold.

"Not Worth a Continental"

I N MORE RECENT TIMES, to finance our Revolutionary War, the Continental Congress issued paper money in great quantities. Over a period of about four and a half years, the Continental currency fell from a value of one paper dollar per one gold dollar, to about 1,000 to one.

William Gouge, writing in 1833, quotes one member of the Continental Congress: "Do you think, gentlemen, that I will consent to load my constituents with taxes, when we can send to our printer, and get a wagon load of money, (25 sheets) of which will pay for the whole?"

Most of the burden, Mr. Gouge notes, fell on the patriots, "as it was in their hands the paper depreciated. The Tories, who had from the beginning no

Continental currency; a five dollar note issued in 1775.

confidence in it, made it a rule to part with it as soon as possible." Those who trusted the Congress were destroyed; the cynics were not. As a result of this paper money inflation, wrote one of our earliest economists, Pelatiah Webster, "frauds, cheats, and gross dishonesty are introduced, and a thousand idle ways of living attempted in the room of honest industry, economy, and diligence, which have heretofore enriched and blessed the country. . . .

"While we rejoice in the riches and strengths of our country, we have reason to lament with tears of the deepest regret, the *most* pernicious shifts of property which the irregularities of our finances introduced, and the many of thousands of fortunes which were ruined by it; the generous, patriotic spirits suffered the injury: the idle and avaricious derived benefit from said confusion."

The phrase "Not worth a Continental" records the fate of this paper currency.

The Best Medium
of Exchange

During most of the nineteenth century, we had a functioning gold standard. Combined with classical liberal economic policies and limited government, this set the stage for the greatest economic growth in history.

Although many Americans today see sound money as the exception, and paper as the rule, the opposite is true. Even the American dollar had a connection with gold up until 1971. Since the severing of that tie, the debasement of the dollar has accelerated, with the money supply doubling. Prices have more than doubled in the last ten years, not to mention the economic distortions that accompanied this inflation.

U.S. three dollar gold piece from 1854.

There is no law of economics stating that only gold can be used as money in a free society. But gold has served as the principal medium of exchange throughout history because its value does not depend on a government fulfilling its promises, especially in times of crisis. Gold is scarce; it is portable; it is easily divisible; it is durable; it is desirable for non-monetary purposes; and it is impossible to counterfeit.[1]

Paper money's worth depends on the promises of government, and it is all too easy to reproduce. Combine these with the human flaws that seem to

---

[1] Although this booklet was written to encourage the establishment of a gold coin standard, it does not suggest the discouragement of other, non-fraudulent commodity money.

be especially common in politicians and central bankers, and you have the fact that no fiat currency can serve as a stable medium of exchange for more than a short time. Until we recognize this, constructive monetary reform is impossible.

Once we do recognize it, we can begin to make progress toward a modern gold standard. Refinement of past systems is necessary because—having been monopolized by government—they have suffered from the inevitable expediency of the politicians.

CROSS OF PAPER

"YOU SHALL NOT CRUCIFY Mankind upon a cross of gold," said inflationist William Jennings Bryan. But mankind, especially poorer and more vulnerable people, is oppressed by paper money, not by gold. It was for this reason that Thomas Jefferson and Andrew Jackson—the presidents who were our greatest defenders of the common man—were such unalterable opponents of paper money.

"[Gold] is the most perfect medium," said Jefferson, "because it will preserve its own level; because, having intrinsic and universal value, it can never die in our hands. . . . [Paper money] is liable to be abused, has been, is, and forever will be abused, in every country in which it is permitted."

Expansion of the money supply through "spurious paper currency," noted Jackson, "is always attended by a loss to the laboring classes."

"Of all the contrivances for cheating the laboring classes of mankind," added Daniel Webster, "none has been found more effectual than that which deludes them with paper money."

"The rise of prices that follows an expansion of [paper money]," wrote William Gouge, President Jackson's Treasury advisor, in 1833, "does not affect all descriptions of labor and commodities, at the same time, to an equal degree. . . . Wages appear to be among the last things that are raised. . . . The working man finds all the articles he uses in his family rising in price, while the money rate of his own wages remains the same."

During the greenback paper money inflation of the Civil War, prices rose 183 percent, while wages

U.S. five dollar gold piece from 1900.

went up only 54 percent. During the World War I inflation, prices rose 135 percent, and wages increased only 88 percent. The same is true today.

Says Dr. Murray Rothbard: "When greenback-dominated prices rose during the Civil War, gold prices (gold still circulating, especially in California) didn't go up, so that it was obvious to everyone what the cause of inflation was: and it wasn't speculators, businessmen, slackers, etc., all of whom were involved in gold as well as paper."

How Our Money
Was Ruined

THE TRANSITION OF THE United States from a gold coin standard to a managed fiat currency was slow and uneven, but it came about as the result of deliberate Congressional decisions. Most intellectuals over the past half century haven't challenged the transition; they have promoted it. We have come far from the days of the Founding Fathers, who decreed death—in the Mint Act of 1792—for any officer or employee of the Mint who debased the coinage of the United States.

"Without the automatic check of a gold standard," wrote Professor William Quirk in the *New Republic*, "the Nixon and Carter administrations were able, in a remarkably short time, to turn the once awesome dollar into Monopoly money."

Fortunately for us and our children, reform of the monetary system can occur quickly, with minimal turmoil, if we are only willing to accept the fundamentals of a free society, which would permit a new monetary system to function, and a long-abused economy to recover swiftly. Here is a short history of our monetary decline.

1. THE GOLD COIN STANDARD

The gold coin standard, although imperfectly adhered to, permitted startling economic growth combined with falling prices in the nineteenth century. In the 67 years since the abolition of the gold standard, the Consumer Price Index has gone up 625 percent. In the previous 67 years, under an imperfect gold coin standard, the CPI increased 10 percent. In his 1848 *Communist Manifesto,* Karl Marx urged: "Centralization of credit in the hands of the state, by means of a national bank with state capital and an exclusive monopoly." Sixty-five years later, the United States followed his advice, and passed the Federal Reserve Act of 1913.

Almost 100 years before, Daniel Webster had argued against a similar central bank:

"What sort of an institution, Sir, is this? It looks less like a bank than a department of government. It will be properly the paper-money department. . . .

"Whenever bank-notes are not convertible into gold and silver at the will of the holder, they become of less value than gold and silver. All experiments on this subject have come to the same result. It is so clear, and has been so universally admitted, that it would be a waste of time to dwell on it. The depreciation may not be sensibly perceived the first day, or the first week, it takes place. It will first be discerned in what is called the rise of specie; it will next be seen in the increased price of all commodities. The circulating medium of a commercial community must be that which is also the circulating medium of other commercial communities, or must be capable of being converted into that medium without loss. It must be able, not only to pass in payments and receipts among individuals of the same society and nation, but to adjust and discharge the balance of exchanges between different nations. It must be something which has a value abroad, as well as at home, and by which foreign as well as domestic debts can be satisfied. The precious metals alone answer these purposes. They alone, therefore, are money, and whatever else is to perform the offices of money must be their representative, and capable of being turned into them at will. . . .

"It will be altogether unpardonable in us, if, with this as well as all other experience before us, we continue to pursue a system which must inevitably lead us through depreciation of currency, papermoney, tender-laws, and all the contemptible and miserable contrivances of disordered finance and national insolvency, to complete and entire bankruptcy in the end."

2. The Gold Bullion Standard

Although it did not become apparent for decades, the Federal Reserve Act made possible the massive inflation necessary to finance our tragic entrance into World War I. The 1921 depression was one result of this inflation.

More Federal Reserve inflation during the 1920s, combined with economic interventionism by both Republican and Democratic administrations, caused and perpetuated the Great Depression of the 1930s.

By that 1913 law, a 40 percent gold cover for Federal Reserve notes and 35 percent for Federal Reserve deposits were required. The fact that it was not 100 percent showed that the central bankers planned more inflation.

If a country inflates under a gold standard, gold flows out of the Treasury, hamstringing the government. Since a gold standard enables the average person to restrain the government's attempts to inflate, control the economy, run up deficits, and fight senseless wars, the central planners had to eliminate this fundamental American freedom to own gold. This was accomplished with the Gold Reserve Act of 1934, which outlawed private ownership of gold, prohibited the use of "gold clause" contracts, and abolished the gold coin standard. The law created the gold bullion standard, destined to last for only ten years.

Since 1933, the dollar has lost more than 93 percent of its value in terms of gold.

Although many, even in the 1930s, predicted that abandoning a redeemable currency would lead to a non-productive, chaotic economy, the bullion standard was only one step in the wrong direction. Its inevitable results were not immediately apparent.

The politicians readily accepted the inflationist arguments of the intellectuals, since it was in the interest of power-hungry politicians to destroy the system that gave the people, not the politicians, power over the monetary system. As a result, control was handed over to the bankers and bureaucrats, as well as the politicians themselves.

"The Federal Reserve System was formed," claims Professor Paul Samuelson, "in the face of strong banker opposition."

In fact, the Fed was instituted at the behest of the American Bankers Association and the nation's biggest bankers, such as J. P. Morgan and Paul Warburg, to protect their industry against bank failures and to provide a more "elastic" currency. That is, to promote inflation that benefits bankers and big corporations. The latter were also active in promoting banking "reform" through the National Civic Federation, the big companies' trade association. In opposition, notes Richard Johns, stood the National Association of Manufacturers, then primarily composed of small businessmen. As the chairman of one giant railroad put it, adds Johns, the Federal Reserve was needed to provide "intelligent control over the credit situation through a board of leading bankers under government supervision and control."

"There is no subtler nor surer means of overturning the existing basis of society than to debauch the currency," Keynes had written in 1919. "The process engages all the hidden forces of economic law on the side of destruction, and does it in a manner which not one man in a million is able to diagnose."

The establishment of a gold bullion standard did not, by itself, destroy the monetary system. But it sowed more seeds of destruction. Prohibiting the private ownership of gold and making "gold-clause" contracts illegal not only violated constitutional rights, it eliminated a free people's ultimate protection from spendthrift and untrustworthy government.

Most Americans acquiesced in the seizure of private gold, and in increasing government intervention in the economy. Notes Dr. Murray Rothbard: "One reason why it was so easy for the government to confiscate everyone's gold in 1933 was that by that time, Establishment propaganda had worked to the extent that few people were actually *using* gold coins in their daily lives. Not using gold much, they didn't think they missed it. This should be a lesson to us all, that if we manage to get a return to gold, we should try to cultivate among the public a considerable daily use."

The corporate and social welfare system, which was to necessitate the elimination of any gold standard, was well established by the late 1930s. Its maturity, combined with foreign military welfare, would require the total abolition decades later of any restraints on the politicians and their power to run the printing presses indiscriminately.

After the Second World War, we remained a wealthy nation, especially in comparison to the nations ravaged by war. And gold continued to flow in, until 1948. The flow continued, not because of wise monetary decisions, but in spite of them. The lifting of wartime economic controls, in the absence of most of today's regulations and some of our taxes, along with a 75 percent cut in Federal spending, led to real growth, whereas other countries were much less stable.

The massive accumulation of gold in the U.S. Treasury at the time provided an excellent opportunity for the establishment of a full gold coin standard. This would have prevented all the subsequent inflation that has so undermined our freedom and our prosperity, as Congressman Howard Buffett of Nebraska pointed out at the time. He introduced legislation to accomplish this, but it was ignored.

Instead, our leaders went to Bretton Woods, drew up an agreement with bankers from other nations, and set America on a disaster course.

3. The Gold Exchange Standard

The monetary reforms drawn up at Bretton Woods, New Hampshire, in July 1944, were supposed to be permanent. The agreement lasted barely 27 years.

Harry Dexter White, Director of Monetary Research for the Treasury, was the U.S. representative. (Mr. White was later identified as a high-level fellow traveler of the Communist Party.)

At this United Nations Monetary and Financial Conference, the gold bullion standard was altered, since it did not allow monetary destruction at a quick enough pace. Although the new system was hailed as an improvement, it was simply a way to institutionalize long-term inflation and further transfer power to the politicians and bankers. It was also the means to finance the interventionist foreign policy so recently adopted, by creating money and credit out of thin air. Political pain and economic disruption at home were to be eased by exporting much of the inflation.

Forty-four nations agreed to the establishment of a World Bank and an International Monetary Fund, which began operations in 1946 under a "new" gold exchange standard. This permitted dollars—said to be "as good as gold"—to be substituted for gold as the international reserve currency.

The stated purpose of the new system was "to maintain exchange stability and stimulate world economic activity"—nothing more than an international Federal Reserve System. The dollar, valued at 1/35th of an ounce of gold, was to be honored in payment of international debts.

The plan seemed workable to many, especially since we owned over 700 million ounces of gold: 75 percent of all the government-held gold in the world. What the proponents did not understand was the nature of politicians and others who strive for power. Human action rarely follows the recipe of the cookbook economic interventionists.

With this agreement, gold ceased to flow back and forth to settle balance of payment differences, thus eliminating an essential feature of a sound monetary system.

Our advisors should have known better; the gold exchange standard had been tried once before. It was in 1922 that a similar charade was tried at the

Genoa Convention in a desperate attempt to hide the bad effects of inflation without stopping the inflation itself. In this agreement pounds sterling and dollars were to be accepted as reserve currencies and treated as if they were literally gold.

The Genoa agreement did nothing to thwart the pain and suffering that followed with the depression of the 1930s. The dollars and pounds remained in the country of origin and were loaned out again, thus "beating" inflation—in spite of the fact that they were recorded as assets (gold) in another central bank as backing for their currency. When this shaky pyramid of credit crumbled in 1929 the depression was ushered in. Jacques Rueff in his outstanding book *The Monetary Sin of the West* describes how dangerous the gold exchange standard is. "The unending feedback of the dollars and pounds received by the European countries to the overseas countries from which they had come, reduced the international monetary system to a mere child's game in which one party had agreed to return the loser's stake after each game of marbles." This is not unlike the recycling of Arab oil money to New York then to Third World nations, then back to the Arab nations in payment for oil, etc., in a managed fiat currency system.

The fact that the later gold exchange standard lasted longer than the one set up in the 1920s, and that the patchwork monetary policy of the managed fiat currency has delayed the inevitable, should not make us complacent. The eventual debt liquidation may differ from that of the 1930s, but it cannot be prevented. I fear that the delay and the sophistication with which we inflate will only end in a bigger and more vicious economic upheaval—probably a totally depreciated currency with runaway price inflation—unless we restore sanity to the monetary system.

For the gold exchange standard to have worked, the men in charge of the American dollar would have had to refuse to expand the money supply. No one, of course, can be trusted with such a responsibility. The temptation to create new money is always too great.

Even though the government always claims it is creating wealth for the unfortunate, a little reflection makes it obvious that no wealth can be created by duplicating monetary units. Wealth can, and is, transferred from one to another, but no new wealth is created. And the transfer is usually from the less-well-off to the well-to-do.

Once the stage was set for deliberate monetary expansion to "stimulate" the domestic economy and to fund international balance of payments deficits, the disintegration of the gold exchange standard was only a matter of time. No one knew the exact timing, but Henry Hazlitt and Congressman Howard Buffett predicted, when the agreement was signed, the exact results. The purpose of Bretton Woods, noted Hazlitt in 1944, is "to make resort to inflation easy, smooth, and above all respectable."

It takes a long time, even with extravagant monetary expansion, to convince the world that a country with more than 700 million ounces of gold would default on its monetary commitments. The claim that America's industrial might stood behind the dollar was revealed as hollow, however, when the IOUs were called in.

The weakening position of the American dollar was hidden for most of the 1950s, but in the 1960s it became obvious to everyone. Patches were applied to the system, but they had no permanent effect.

The gold reserves the Federal Reserve System had to maintain against Federal Reserve notes had been decreased, in 1945, from 35 percent to 25 percent. To continue the inflation fraud, this figure had to be reduced to zero. In 1968 it was. In 1965 gold reserve requirements for Federal Reserve deposit liabilities were removed. Treasury gold sales, a two-tier gold pricing system, and the international "gold pool" did nothing to restore monetary order or instill confidence in the declining dollar, except for desperately short periods of time. Nothing worked because government cannot repeal the laws of human nature or of economics. Politicians simply can't be trusted with the money machine. The Bretton Woods system died, at the ripe old age of 27, on August 15, 1971, when President Nixon closed the "gold window," and refused to redeem overseas dollars for gold. The road to rampant inflation was opened, to the delight of the bureaucrats, politicians, international bankers, multinational corporations, and some labor leaders. The age of the managed fiat currency was born.

4. THE MANAGED FIAT CURRENCY STANDARD

As could be expected, this "new" standard (actually as old as the French Assignat or the American Continental) inspired little confidence in the international community. Most Americans, unfortunately, ignored it. No efforts were made to restore monetary order, except by a few hard-money groups, which were of necessity outside the Establishment. Those who had benefitted from inflation were not about to repudiate the corrupt system that had brought them affluence and power.

When Nixon declared that foreign holders of dollars could no longer exchange them for gold, the gold exchange standard came to a miserable end. It had made possible the inflation which financed the Vietnam War and the Great Society, as well as massive business malinvestments. But the worst was yet to come.

The dollar died on August 15, 1971; after that date, it had no independent value for anyone. The new rules, with the dollar now simply a managed fiat currency, ushered in even greater inflation, economic turmoil, and set the stage for total loss of confidence in the dollar. When the price of gold triples in a year, we see the loss of confidence in graphic terms. A similar run-up in all prices can occur when the average American housewife expresses the same loss of confidence in the dollar's integrity as the Eurodollar holder. This will happen eventually, and perhaps in the near future, although no one knows exactly when.

The Smithsonian Agreement, which followed the closing of the "gold window," was even worse than the previous arrangements. And it was doomed to even quicker failure.

Since 1971, the price of gold has increased by more than twentyfold. The CPI has gone up 79 percent, M1 by 63 percent, M2 by 102 percent, and the annual trade deficit by 1,146 percent. All of this is testimony to an age that believes wealth can come to us without productive effort.

As Samuel Johnson wrote in *The Rambler,* "The reigning error of mankind is, that we are not content with the conditions on which the goods of life are granted." Many shrink from the contrast between the work ethic and the welfare ethic, between honest money and dishonest money, between reality and fantasy.

THE STAGE IS SET

WITH THE DEATH OF the dollar, the time is ripe for the institution of a trustworthy monetary system. The times demand it, and so does the survival of our economic and political order.

The task is not difficult, if we ignore—for once—the political pressures from the special interests whose demands are fulfilled through inflation of the money supply. Inflation, whether for the benefit of big companies, bankers, bureaucrats, monopoly wages, transfer payments, or political careers, must be ended. And, as Henry Hazlitt points out, the solution is not difficult: "To stop inflation we must stop inflating (the money supply)."

If we expect to reverse the destruction of our economy, we must try to understand the motives of those who promote inflation.

Many big business people, bankers, union leaders, politicians, and professors all grew to love inflation, as they saw in it a chance to pursue their goals. Sometimes these were purely materialistic; at other times they embodied the lust for power. In both cases they were immoral.

The political pressure to inflate is the main reason for confirmed expansion of the money supply. Monetization of Federal debt, with the Federal Reserve turning government bonds into money, is a convenient and politically easy way to pay the bills run up by Congress, without resorting to a tax rate that would literally provoke revolt.

Everyone in Congress talks about a balanced budget, but few consistently vote for one. Each Member always hopes that it will be the other man's projects that will be cut, not his own. Recently, I watched one conservative Congressman vote for a gigantic pork-barrel spending bill. Knowing that the money would either have to be taxed from the people or printed up, I asked him how he could do it. "Oh, I know it's a terrible thing," he answered. "But I might need a project for my district someday." Liberals we expect to be big spenders, but it's disheartening to see people who should know better voting for business and farm subsidies, while expressing horror—rightly at

German inflation notes; center is a one-billion mark note from 1923.

Comprehensive Employment and Training Act (CETA). Without a far-reaching change of attitude, the budget won't be balanced, the printing presses will continue to run, the dollar will be further debased, and prices—as a consequence—will continue to rise relentlessly.

Is Business To Blame?

Some say business profits are the cause of inflation. But profits—in a voluntary market—are only an indication of efficiency and service to consumers. Legitimate profits have nothing whatsoever to do with inflation.

But big business' demand for "easy money" certainly has been a significant reason for monetary expansion. Alan Greenspan, for example, claims that credit expansion to supply more than $600 billion in Federally guaranteed loans, all of which are for the benefit of business, is the most significant contributing factor to our inflation.

When I studied the amount of inflation since 1970 and the proportion of Federal deficits in those years that needed to be monetized—created out of thin air—I came up with some startling figures. It is possible that only twenty percent of the inflation, the expansion of the money supply, was necessitated by deficit spending. *Eighty percent* of the inflation, therefore, may have been for "stimulation" of the economy to aid big business and big banking. Whatever the motive, these institutions profit from the depreciation of the dollar.

Are Banks To Blame?

Some of the large banks, which have been promi-nent promoters of fiat currency, have certainly benefitted from inflation. Their "profits" have been enhanced, since somebody has to broker all the new money created by government, and pass it on to the large corporations. The international bankers are delighted to do so.

The banks also have the privilege of creating checking account money, known as demand deposits. The banks create this money in the process of making loans—loans for which they charge interest. Much of our money consists of bank-created demand deposits.

Inflation bestows benefits, as well as wreaking havoc. Wealth is transferred from one group to another. Although the transfer has haphazard elements, it goes from the middle class and the poor to the government, the bankers, and the large corporations. This is the immoral process that must be stopped.

Are Unions To Blame?

Unions are accused of causing inflation. But unions cannot create new money and credit, so they cannot be held directly responsible for inflation. But just as business can exert pressure on government to inflate, so can monopoly wage increases. A good example is the credit the government created to bailout the Chrysler Corporation, largely to finance a labor contract that pays the employees twice the average industrial wage. But unions, like businesses, can only persuade government to inflate if the inflation mechanism is in place. A redeemable currency would make this impossible.

Inflation and the
Business Cycle

THE BUSINESS CYCLE, which Marx maintained is inherent in capitalism, is actually caused by government inflation. "New money is issued by the banking system, under the aegis of government," says Dr. Murray Rothbard, "and loaned to business. To businessmen, the new funds seem to be genuine investments. But these do not, like free market investments, arise from voluntary savings. The new money is invested by businessmen in various projects, and paid out to workers and other factors as higher wages and prices. As the new money filters down to the whole economy, the people tend to reestablish their old voluntary consumption/savings proportions. In short, if people wish to save and invest about 20 percent of their income and consume the rest, new bank money loaned to business at first makes the saving proportion look higher. When the new money seeps down to the public, it reestablishes its old 20–80 proportion, and many investments are now revealed to be wasteful. Inflationary credit distorted the market, and misled the businessmen. Liquidation of the wasteful investments of the inflationary boom constitutes the depression phase of the business cycle."

Expansion of the money supply also temporarily lowers interest rates, which creates malinvestment as well.

Interventionist economists carelessly criticize the spreading of economic growth throughout a free-market society as the "trickle-down theory." But inflation, by trickling, then rushing, through society, spreads economic misery among the poor, working, and middle classes, while enriching the special interests. It is *this* "trickling-down" that deserves condemnation from everyone concerned about poverty.

"An increase in the money supply confers no social benefits whatsoever," says Dr. Hans Sennholz. "It merely redistributes income and wealth, disrupts and misguides economic production, and as such constitutes a powerful weapon in a conflict society."

Whoever gets the new money first benefits the most. But the favored industry becomes dependent on new injections of government credit, and therefore forms a powerful special interest lobby to argue its viewpoint in Washington. Thus does inflation encourage the breakdown of society into warring factions.

THE GUILT OF THE ECONOMISTS

ANOTHER OUTRAGE ASSOCIATED with inflation is the endorsement of the process by most economists. It's bad enough to see the beneficiaries promote wealth transfer through inflation, but to have the majority of twentieth-century economists do so as well is tragic. Some do so because they realize that their power and prestige depends on their giving an intellectual rationale to the acts of the inflation elite. But many do not benefit directly, and their motives may be good. But whether they promote inflation to help the poor, to help the rich, or just believe it is in everyone's interest, the results are horrendous.

The interventionist economists who endorse inflation fail to accept the subjective theory of value, as formulated by the free-market economists. This

A ten-million pengo inflation note from Hungary, 1946.

theory, without which it is impossible to dispel old economic myths, holds that the value of an economic good exists only in the minds of individuals, and that it can change with circumstances and over time. Prices, and the production decisions which they determine, cannot come from mathematical models in computers.

Even the monetarists endorse sustained inflation, albeit at a lesser rate than is presently the case. The best-known monetarist, Dr. Milton Friedman, says the Fed should expand the money supply at three to five percent a year, the actual figure being less important than the absence of fluctuations.

But even this amount of inflation inevitably introduces malinvestment as those getting the new money put it to uses that only later recessions show to have been unproductive. The Friedman approach may produce milder booms and recessions, and less human suffering, than present policy, but it nevertheless is inflationary and a product of the old, discredited idea that government, rather than the market, should be planning the economy. Worst of all, it establishes the principle of government control of the money supply and would allow an increase in the inflation percentage if "needed."

The politicians and many bankers, union leaders, businessmen, and bureaucrats who profit from inflation are glad, of course, to have the intellectuals justify their fraud. It's unfortunate that economists who promote inflation are today called liberals, since a more illiberal and reactionary policy could hardly be imagined. They are also inaccurately called progressives, since inflation is an archaic device.

Although today's coin clippers and debasers use sophisticated monetary arrangements to legitimatize their acts, this makes no difference. Political, economic, and monetary turmoil still result.

To promote inflation, the well-intended economist must blind himself to the economic dislocations and distortions that occur. Economic calculation becomes increasingly difficult every day, yet the promoters of inflation will not accept their responsibility.

Inflation often leads to price and wage controls, which destroy the pricing system, the planning mechanism of the free economy. If these economists understood this, the only reason they could promote inflation would be to destroy freedom.

Nobel prize-winner Friedrich von Hayek wrote in 1959 that "It is no accident that inflationary policies are generally advocated by those who want more government control. . . . The increased dependence of the individual upon government which inflation produces and the demand for more government action to which this leads may for the socialist be an argument in its favor. . . . All who wish to stop the drift toward increasing control should concentrate their efforts on monetary policies."

The Alternative
to Inflation

INFLATION DESTROYS the incentive to save, especially when there are government ceilings on interest, as with savings accounts. Our tax system—taxing illusionary income—worsens this, and we can expect to see a smaller and smaller amount saved by Americans. Inflation steals from those who still believe in thrift, and robs pensions and retirement funds. How can any reasonable economist promote inflation with these facts staring him in the face?

We have an opportunity to present to our people an alternative to the old, the failed, the tool of special interests: an alternative that is modern, that works, that benefits everyone. That alternative must be one that rejects inflation and dishonest money. *It is a redeemable gold dollar.*

MONEY AND THE
CONSTITUTION

"IT IS APPARENT from the whole context of the Constitution, as well as the history of the times which gave birth to it," said Andrew Jackson, "that it was the purpose of the Convention to establish a currency consisting of the precious metals."

"The loss which America has sustained since the peace," noted James Madison in *Federalist Number 44*, "from the pestilent effects of paper money on the necessary confidence between man and man, on the necessary confidence in public councils, on the industry and morals of the people, and on the character of republican government, constitutes an enormous debt against the State chargeable with this unadvised measure, which must long remain unsatisfied; or rather an accumulation of guilt, which can be expiated no otherwise than by a voluntary sacrifice on the altar of justice of the power which has been the instrument of it."

"The emitting of paper money is wisely prohibited to the State Governments," said Alexander Hamilton, "and the spirit of the prohibition ought not to be disregarded by the United States' Government."

Not only is inflation the result of the political demands of special interest groups, the career desires of politicians, and the ill-conceived motives of economists, it is also clearly unconstitutional.

Money of real value, gold or silver, was clearly intended by the Founding Fathers, as evidenced in their writings and in the Constitution. Their

Legal tender Colonial paper money;
six dollars note from the Colony of Maryland.

abhorrence of paper money stemmed from their experience with the Continental, and irredeemable Colonial paper money. That same abhorrence is becoming evident today as well, which is a healthy sign for those of us interested in developing a sound money system.

Morality and
Transfer Payments

I F FOR NO OTHER REASON, inflation should be rejected on the basis of morality. Inflation is taxation by deceit. Government deceives the people as to the tax burden, and who is bearing it. The working and middle classes are gradually impoverished, while the poor are ground further down.

Wealth is transferred to the rich, from the hardworking and thrifty to the conniving and foxy.

Inflation should be rejected by any society, but especially by one claiming a Christian-Hebraic heritage. Not only is wealth transferred from one group of citizens to another, in a giant anti-Robin Hood operation, but authority is transferred from citizens to the government.

Monetary and economic decisions are increasingly taken from individuals and transferred to politicians, bureaucrats, and central bankers. To enforce the transfer, government officials accumulate power through legislation and regulation. Coercion becomes commonplace; voluntary decisions are called detrimental to the "whole," and freedom is gradually destroyed.

Without a moral society, honest money cannot exist. Without morality and honest money, a free society cannot exist. An immoral society and dishonest money go hand in hand.

CITIZEN CONTROL
OF MONEY

THE REPUDIATION of debt through debasement of the currency is an ancient trick for not paying the bills. Default is at least done in the open. Inflation is much more destructive and dishonest, especially when the largest debtor—the government—controls the money supply.

Adam Smith notes in *The Wealth of Nations* that "When national debts have once been accumulated to a certain degree, there is scarce, I believe, a single instance of their having been fairly and completely paid. The liberation of the public revenue, if it has even been brought about at all, has always been brought about by a bankruptcy; sometimes by an avowed one, but always by a real one, though frequently by a pretended payment."

Over the centuries, governments have used the theft of inflation to finance unpopular endeavors. In a free nation, adventurism at home with massive transfer programs, or abroad with no-win wars, would be impossible, since the people would simply refuse to pay the higher taxes, or loan the government the necessary money. On the other hand, a popular cause would elicit the necessary funding through loans, donations, or taxes.

DAY OF RECKONING

THE DAY OF RECKONING is upon us. The people now recognize the inflation hoax for what it is, and are demanding reform. Congress' responsibility is clear, but the choices are varied.

We can continue down the rutted road of the past half century, which will lead to monetary collapse and perhaps a new currency, as in Israel recently, and hundreds of times in other countries since 1900. But if the new currency is a fiat one, nothing will have been changed.

We could take the monetarists' advice, and keep on inflating, but at a lower rate. But if 4 percent is good, what's wrong with 5 percent or 50 percent? If the growth in the money supply is to coincide with economic growth, what if there is a decline? Then the monetarists openly call for massive inflation.

A ten dollar Confederate note issued from the Richmond bank.

They still cling to the idea that wealth and productivity are somehow created by an increase in the number of monetary units. Some otherwise excellent friends of freedom promote this theory, but it offers nothing but economic and intellectual confusion.

Whether the Federal Reserve, the Congress, or the bankers control the money system makes no difference. All inevitably abuse this control, which is why we need a money controlled only by the people.

The only moral, constitutional, and economically productive alternative is the 100 percent redeemable gold coin standard, which puts the citizen in control.

Some monetarists answer that gold has been abused in the past by government. But this is hardly an argument for a paper standard, since paper is infinitely more abusable. This is no different from arguing that since government has abused the right of freedom of speech, we should have no First Amendment.

Free Market Money?

PERHAPS IN THE FUTURE we need to consider free market money, allowing consumers to decide about their money the way they decide about everything else. Hans Sennholz and Friedrich von Hayek argue for this system. And it existed at one time in our country.

In California, during the 1840s and 1850s, many privately minted gold coins circulated. The practice was outlawed in 1864, "but as late as 1914," points out Antony Sutton, "the U.S. Treasury was still trying to halt circulation of private gold pieces in San Francisco." Why were such coins still circulating? Because the private mints maintained higher standards than the government mint. Often, points out Dr. Sutton, they were one percent heavier than Federal issues, "to protect the user from metal loss by abrasion while the coin was in circulation." Private mints held to a higher standard because they were protected only by their reputation. They could not force consumers to take substandard money by the force of law, as government can.

The North financed the Civil War with hundreds of millions of dollars of irredeemable Greenback notes, and as a result, prices more than doubled from 1861 to 1865.

The first legal tender notes were issued in 1862 and came to be called "greenbacks."

During the Greenback inflation, people in California continued to use gold as their money. "In California, as in other states," points out Frank Taussig, "paper was legal tender. . ." that is, people could be forced to accept it. Although there was no antipathy towards the Federal government, people believed strongly in gold. "Every debtor had the legal right to pay off his debts in depreciated paper. But if he did so, he was a marked man (the creditor was likely to post him publicly in the newspapers) and he was virtually boycotted. Throughout the period, paper was not used in California."

LEGAL TENDER LAWS

AT THE VERY LEAST, we must repeal the legal tender laws that force people to accept the government's money, and set up a gold coin standard impossible for the politicians and bankers to debase. We should also end the legal monopoly on banking, allow free entry, and make it an open, competitive business like any other.

Legal tender laws tell people what they must accept as payment. If government issues only sound money, such laws are unnecessary. But they become oppressive when government debases the money. When this happens, legal tender laws favor debtors over creditors. But only present debtors are benefitted. Future would-be borrowers are penalized by the scarcity of credit, created by inflation and legal tender laws.

The central bank never set out to protect the integrity of our money. In fact, the Fed set out to destroy it by institutionalizing inflation. The gold coin standard was doomed and today's inflation made inevitable the day the Federal Reserve was created.

If government is to exercise monetary responsibility, it must be in establishing a 100 percent gold redeemable currency. And, notes William Rees-Mogg, "the prize is very great. . . . Good money (gold) restores reality to the payment for work and to saving. It permits not only the businessman but every citizen to plan his economic life ahead, and fulfill his own plans. It gives a real target not only to great ambitions but also to humble ones. It provides a solid platform for democratic government. It brings inflation to an end. Above all, good money would restore the sanity, the limited and proportionate character, of economic life. It would rid the world not only of inflation, but of the economic hubris which is worse than inflation itself."

An Historical Precedent

ONGRESS MADE THE GREENBACK notes redeemable in gold in 1879, and the effect of this action can help us plan for a similar action in the future.

By the end of the Civil War, a Greenback dollar was worth less than 50 cents in gold. But as it became obvious that Congress would redeem them in Constitutional money, gold, they became worth more. The government also stopped inflating.

By 1868 it only took $138 in Greenbacks to buy $100 in gold, and by 1874, $111.

Late in 1875, Congress passed a law saying that on January 1, 1879, Greenbacks would be redeemable in gold on a one-to-one basis. And the notes were to be retired gradually.

As the date approached, says Dr. Donald Kemmerer, "the price of $100 in gold in greenbacks declined from $111.50 in 1876 to $104.70 in 1877 and $101.10 in 1878. On December 17, 1878, two weeks before the official specie resumption day, the price of $100 in gold reached $100 in Greenbacks."

Dr. Kemmerer summarized the rather placid experience:

"The *New York Herald* relegated the story to page 3, and headlined it 'Resumption—An Unexciting Event Throughout the Country.' There were flags flying from many buildings on Wall Street, and a Navy Yard battery at ten o'clock officially announced the opening of the New York Subtreasury. This was the *only* place in the country actually required to exchange gold for greenbacks. Banks everywhere prepared to redeem greenbacks, however, as a matter of convenience. When the doors of the New York Subtreasury opened at ten, there were fifteen clerks inside ready to serve the expected crowd. 'Behind the glass were piled immense quantities of gold in coins all the way from dollars to double eagles.' Actually the 'crowd' at the opening consisted of only one person who demanded gold for his $210 of greenbacks. No one else appeared for another half hour. There were only about 15 or 20 people altogether before half past one. But then the clerks had redeemed $3000 in gold, the most frequently requested amount being $50. Technically $50 was the smallest amount the Subtreasury was permitted to pay out under the Resumption Act. Some people came to the Subtreasury merely to collect monies owing to them by the government. Each was asked whether he wanted to be paid in gold or greenbacks, and most of them preferred greenbacks which were easier to handle.

"One young man called at the Subtreasury and asked for $5000 in gold. He got a bag of it (weighing about 17 pounds) and handled it somewhat carelessly. Gold eagles were soon rolling in every direction. After gathering and recounting them he returned the gold and asked for 'some currency that will not roll about.'"

The End—or
the Beginning

G OVERNMENT'S ONLY LEGITIMATE reason for existence is to protect innocent life and property
from aggression, foreign or domestic. When it delib-
erately destroys the money, government is acting
perversely, by harming innocent life and property.
Short of intentional war, inflation is the most immoral
act political leaders can commit.

The legalized counterfeiting which is inflation
must be ended—now.

The road to monetary destruction has been long
and circuitous, but we are coming to the end of it.
Sixty-seven years of central banking have brought
us to the edge of depression and hyperinflation.

But the foundations have been laid for a new
monetary order. The spirit of freedom, and the desire

for honest money, still run strongly among our people. In 1974 we reversed the unconstitutional 1934 law that barred private ownership of gold. In 1977, gold clause contracts were legalized. In 1979, a bill to repeal the Treasury's power to seize privately held gold was passed by the House.

The minting of U.S. gold medallions has emphasized the importance of the people's right to own gold.

Historic Congressional hearings have been held on the gold standard, and an amendment to establish a gold commission passed both Houses unanimously. The commission, composed of public and private sector representatives, will specifically study the role of gold in the domestic and international monetary systems.

We must also work on halting massive gold sales at below market prices to European central bankers and Arab sheiks. If the administration is still intent on "demonetizing" gold with gold sales, let's at least sell it only in sizes that Americans can afford—one, one half, and one quarter ounce coins.

Eventually, we must repeal the legal tender laws, which work only to the benefit of the government and other large debtors, by forcing creditors to accept depreciated currency, and permit free banking.

Federal Reserve notes must be made 100 percent redeemable in gold as of a fixed date, and at a rate determined by the market price on that date. We also must balance the budget and pledge never again to expand the money supply.

The argument that there's not enough gold to do this is false. With a gold dollar, a car might cost $600 instead of $6,000, but the exact amount of the medium of exchange used wouldn't matter.

"In a free market economy," points out Dr. Hans Sennholz, "it is utterly irrelevant what the total stock of money should be. Any given quantity renders the full services and yields the maximum utility of a medium of exchange. No additional utility can be derived from additions to the money quantity. When the stock is relatively large, the purchasing power

A U.S. $20 gold piece.

of the individual units of money will be relatively small. Conversely, when the stock is small, the purchasing power of the individual units will be relatively large. No wealth can be created and no economic growth can be achieved by changing the quantity of the medium of exchange. It is so obvious and yet so obscured by the specious reasoning of special interest spokesmen that the printing of another ton of paper money does not create new wealth."

Our freedoms are too precious to risk, and if we do not act quickly, we will see them perish just as surely as our currency. This is the ultimate justification for honest money. Freedom cannot long exist without it.

"By a continuing process of inflation, governments can confiscate, secretly and unobserved, an important part of the wealth of their citizens," says John Maynard Keynes. "As the inflation proceeds and the real value of the currency fluctuates wildly from month to month, all permanent relations between debtors and creditors, which form the ultimate foundation of capitalism, become so utterly disordered as to be almost meaningless; and the process of wealth-getting degenerates into a gamble and a lottery.

"Lenin was certainly right. There is no subtler, no surer means of overturning the existing basis of society than to debauch the currency. The process engages all the hidden forces of economic law on the side of destruction, and it does it in a manner which not one man in a million is able to diagnose."[2]

The consequences of monetary destruction are complex, but the solution is not.

Without a moral foundation, a free society cannot survive. The same is true for our money. We will ensure a safe, secure, free, and productive America for ourselves and our descendants only by accepting both a moral defense of the free society and sound money.

"We may amuse ourselves," wrote William Gouge, Treasury advisor to President Andrew Jackson, "by contriving new modes of paper banking. We may suppose that kind of money which has been tried, in various forms, in China, Persia, Hindostan, Tartary, Japan, Russia, Sweden, Denmark, Austria, France, Portugal, England, Scotland, Ireland, Canada, the United States, Brazil, and Buenos Aires,

---

[2] N.B.: "Many people have combed through every word of Lenin, to no avail," writes Dr. Rothbard. "He simply never said it. (To do so he would have to be a lot more familiar with sound economics than he was.) Just another case where Keynes goofed."

and which has everywhere produced mischief, would if we had control of it, be productive of great good. We may say, it is true that paper money has always produced evil, but it is because it has not been properly managed. But, if there is not something essentially bad in fictitious money, there seems to be something in human nature which prevents it from being properly managed. No new experiments are wanted to convince mankind of this truth." Since Mr. Gouge wrote this in 1833, we have had many melancholy examples to add to his list.

Barter and the underground economy, which have already appeared in the U.S., are not the answers. Free people must not accept a retreat into primitive conditions. We must confront the enemies of freedom and honest money with superior ideas and superior determination.

We can prevent the calamity only with the concerted efforts of many dedicated, well-informed citizens willing to put forth a herculean effort—starting today.

The alternative to today's monetary fraud and tomorrow's chaos is readily available to us.

The calamities that accompany monetary chaos have brought dictators to power in other countries. We must prevent this from happening here.

"People fight the gold standard," said Ludwig von Mises, "because they want to substitute national autarky for free trade, war for peace, totalitarian government omnipotence for liberty." It is no coincidence that the nineteenth century, a time of gold coin standards for the most part, was an era of peace. Nor is it a coincidence that the twentieth century combines wars with paper money.

Everyone who believes in freedom must work diligently for sound money, fully redeemable. Nothing else is compatible with the humanitarian goals of peace and prosperity.

INDEX